Originated and designed by
Charles Matheson
and Ben White
and produced by
The Archon Press
70 Old Compton Street
London W1V 5PA

First published in
Great Britain 1979 by
Hamish Hamilton
Children's Books Ltd
Garden House
57–59 Long Acre
London WC2E 9JL

The author wishes to
acknowledge the assistance
of Veronica Tuttin-Brown,
British Museum, London, in
the preparation of this book.

0 241 10334 7

Printed in Great Britain by
W. S. Cowell Ltd
Butter Market, Ipswich

A closer LOOK at

MINOANS

Jane Heath

Illustrated by Ivan Lapper

Hamish Hamilton · London

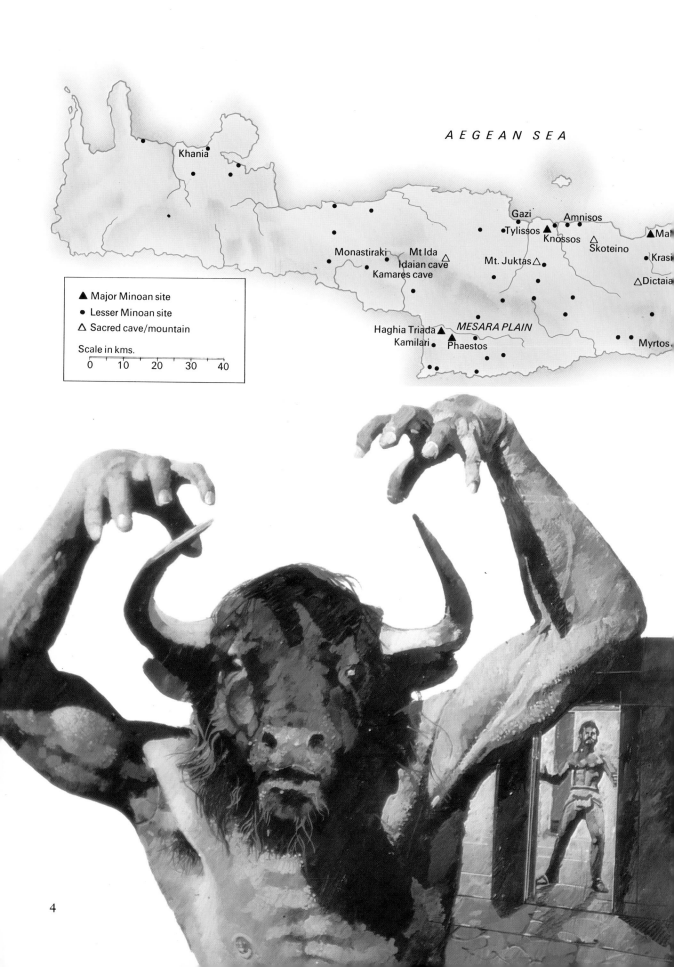

AEGEAN SEA

Khania

Gazi
Amnisos
Tylissos
Knossos
Skoteino
Ma
Monastiraki
Mt Ida
Idaian cave
Kamares cave
Mt. Juktas
Krasi
Dictaia
Haghia Triada
MESARA PLAIN
Kamilari
Phaestos
Myrtos

▲ Major Minoan site
● Lesser Minoan site
△ Sacred cave/mountain

Scale in kms.
0   10   20   30   40

A peaceful land

Crete and her present day neighbours

Position of Crete
Crete is an island in the eastern Mediterranean just south of Greece. At the centre of the ancient world's trading routes and protected by the sea from invasion, Crete was in a very advantageous position.

In 1900 a team of archaeologists led by Sir Arthur Evans began excavations at the site of Knossos in Crete. They unearthed the ruins of a very large and most unusually designed building: a palace. These were among the first discovered traces of a forgotten civilisation so old that even the ancient Greeks only remembered it in folk tales and legends.

Until the nineteenth century Greek legends, like that of Theseus and the Minotaur were the only indication that there had once been a great civilisation on Crete. According to legend, the ruler of Crete, the Minos, had once been powerful enough to exact tribute from Athens on the mainland of Greece. Improbable as this seemed, research following Evans' discovery showed that the Minoans (as called by Evans after their ruler) had in fact once been a great power in the South Aegean.

The earliest settlers are thought to have arrived in Crete in 6000 BC. Where they came from is uncertain, but most scholars believe they originated in Asia Minor. For 4000 years the early Cretans enjoyed a tranquil, if primitive, existence living in caves or simple huts. From about 2000 BC the building of palaces heralded a great leap forward for Minoan civilisation. No one knows what sparked off this rapid development; possibly it was the arrival of immigrants from various other cultures. Being an island, Crete was to a large extent immune from the disruptions, like the Amorite invasion of Syria, that were taking place in the eastern Mediterranean around 1750 BC.

The Minoans strengthened their own security by building up a strong navy. They grew powerful enough to protect themselves and to colonise surrounding islands and possibly even parts of mainland Greece. For about 600 years the Minoan civilisation prospered, but around 1450 BC it declined for reasons not yet fully understood. Volcanic explosions, invasion, social upheaval—probably all contributed to the disappearance of a civilisation which was to lie forgotten for over three thousand years.

Theseus and the Minotaur
When Minos, son of Zeus, was King of Crete, his wife Parsiphae had an affair with a bull and gave birth to a terrible monster with a man's body and a bull's head called the Minotaur.

King Minos built a labyrinth in his palace to house the beast and every eight years compelled the Athenians to send seven youths and seven maidens to be fed to it. Theseus, son of the King of Athens, offered to be one of the seven youths sent.

As soon as Ariadne, Minos' daughter, saw him she fell madly in love. When it was his turn to enter the labyrinth she gave him a ball of thread to unwind behind him. Theseus succeeded in killing the monster and followed the thread safely out of the labyrinth. He then fled from Crete with Ariadne.

This famous legend may be partly true. King Minos may have existed though it is likely that Minos was a title, like Pharaoh or Ceasar, rather than an individual, and the Minoans may have once forced Athens to send people to Crete to be sacrificed to a bull god.

Ninety cities

A country villa
This clay model is typical of the medium-sized dwellings dotted over the Crete countryside. These rectangular one storey houses would have had an open courtyard leading into the five or six-roomed house made of masonry with plaster or stone flagged floors. Some steps led up to the canopied balcony supported on wooden pillars. One large room would have been used as the main living area, and there would have been a storage room for grain and oil.

Crete is a beautiful land. One early seventeenth century visitor described it as 'the garden of the whole Universe'. It is a land of mountains and plains, deep narrow gorges cut into the limestone, and many caves which over the centuries have acted as dwellings, tombs, shrines and places of refuge. In the past the island was heavily wooded; forests covered the lower slopes of the mountains. The coastline, especially in the north where most of the Minoan settlements have been found, is indented with bays and inlets which make natural harbours.

The ancient Greeks regarded the Minoan civilisation as a golden age. Homer, 500 years after it had ceased to exist, said there had once been ninety cities on Crete. Although this is an exaggeration, it demonstrates the legendary prosperity of the Minoans.

Two major natural advantages contributed to their wealth: one was the sea, the other was the very fertile land. People could earn their living from the sea as fishermen or merchant traders. Farmers grew far more vines and olives in the fertile soil than could be consumed by the local population, so they probably exported wine and oil to other lands. Timber was plentiful for building houses and boats, and it may be that this too was an important export. Excess produce seems to have been stored in the palaces and carried there and to the ports in carts drawn by cattle.

Although many people lived in cities and towns, the countryside would have been dotted with the simple houses of peasant

fisherman and farmers. They lived in small, rectangular one-storey buildings with flat roofs, unlike their rich landlords who lived in splendid country villas two or three storeys high. The rich Minoans, like other Near Eastern people at that time, probably had slaves, but there were also free poor people. In the towns, the hovels of the poor mingled with the larger houses of craftsmen, the spacious villas of the nobility and the magnificent palaces of the kings and governors. The houses of the wealthy were covered inside with a veneer of gypsum—a white stone rather like alabaster.

The four Minoan palaces suggest that Crete was divided into independent city states. The biggest and most splendid palace was at Knossos; so the ruler there was probably the most powerful.

Farming land

Crete has always been a fertile land good for agriculture. The land would have been tilled with a wooden plough ready to grow grain, such as wheat and barley. Fruit and vegetables cultivated were figs and dates, olive for oil, grapes for wine, and peas and lentils. The Minoans kept domestic animals like pigs, sheep and goats for meat and milk, and also hunted wild animals like deer, boar and ducks for food.

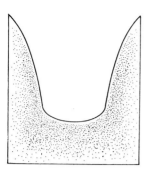

Home of the Minos

Knossos was the capital of Minoan Crete and the largest town in Europe at that time with an estimated population of about 100,000. The palace at Knossos was the centre of Minoan government and power, and the home of the Minos. It is not certain who lived in the other palaces; perhaps members of the royal family, lesser rulers or governors.

The palace excavated by Sir Arthur Evans at Knossos was not the first to be built on that site. Twice the palace was destroyed and twice it was rebuilt. The first palace dates from 2000 BC and though far in advance of its time was simple compared to the later ones. The second, dating from 1700 BC, was built when Minoan civilisation was at its height and was the most magnificent of the three. The third, a reconstruction of the second, shows a strong foreign influence at a time when the Minoan culture was in decline.

The palace was far more than a royal residence; it was an economic and commercial centre. Many rooms were storerooms containing stone boxes and enormous jars (called *pithoi*). These were taller than people and were used chiefly for storing olive oil. Palaces were also centres of craftsmanship and education. Skilled stone masons, potters and artists of all kinds had well-equipped studios and workshops within their walls.

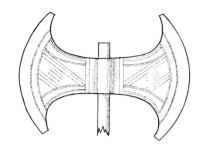

The Palace City of Knossos

The palace consisted of a vast network of rooms, steps and corridors covering several acres. The complex layout is due to each new palace being built on the ruins of the previous one. It may have been this maze-like quality that gave rise to the myth of the labyrinth. The sacred bull's horns (far left) and the double axe head (above) are found as decoration all over Knossos—both seem to have had some religious significance.

The Throne Room
The throne room is decorated
with frescoes of griffins on either
side of the throne. The throne
itself is made of gypsum and set
against the wall. In front of it is a
sunken area, a lustral basin,
probably used for ritual cleansing.

Heart of the labyrinth

The palace at Knossos was built on many levels around a central courtyard. There were entrances on three sides and two grand stairways led from the courtyard to the residential area on the east side, and on the west side to storerooms, shrines and cult rooms, including the throne room. Light penetrated to rooms in the centre of the building by means of light wells. Some of these were open to the sky, others were covered by a raised roof supported by pillars which allowed light in.

Huge wooden pillars supported the flat roofs and upper floors and also gave elegance to the long colonnades. Many of the pillars were painted red and all tapered downwards. This is characteristic of Minoan architecture and may have had religious significance. Two other elements of Minoan religion in architecture are the stylized bull's horns and the double axes. Both appear all over the palace at Knossos; the bull's horns over pillars, arches and in shrines, and the double axe symbol in storerooms and rooms in the residential quarter, where it featured so prominently that the suite of rooms was named by Evans the Hall of Double Axes.

The most striking aspect of the palaces was their wonderful decorations. The early palaces had simple geometric designs in coloured plaster. But in 1700 BC when the second palace at Knossos was built, beautiful pictures were painted on the walls which are now an important source of information about Minoan life. The Minoans loved beauty, elegance and finery and their pictures are full of gaiety. The women in the pictures wear decorated, flounced skirts, and bodices that come to a high point at the back of the neck leaving the breasts exposed. They also wear make-up, intricate jewellery and elaborate hair styles. The men wear short kilts and most have long hair.

The palace layout
This shows the most important rooms surrounding the central courtyard. All this can still be seen at Knossos today.

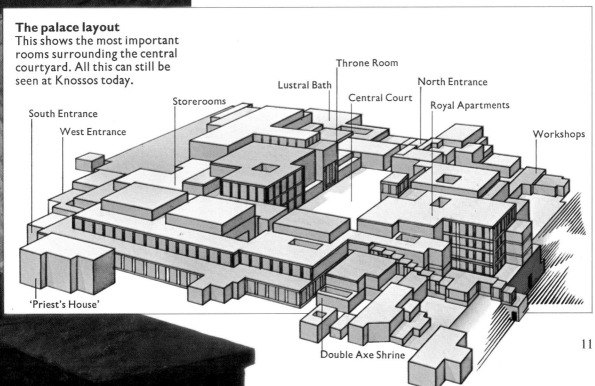

South Entrance

West Entrance

'Priest's House'

Storerooms

Lustral Bath

Throne Room

Central Court

North Entrance

Royal Apartments

Workshops

Double Axe Shrine

Millenia in advance

In certain areas, particularly that of building techniques, the Minoans were far in advance of the rest of Europe. Houses of more than one storey were an achievement in themselves, but that they could build something as complex as any one of the great palaces was absolutely astonishing. There is nothing to compare with them on the mainland.

The Minoans were experts at plastering, veneering and decorating; the artists who created the frescoes worked amazingly quickly to paint their magnificent pictures in the wet plaster before it dried out. The pictures are colourful, skilfully executed and show a remarkable appreciation of the natural world. Minoan artists created graceful, life-like pictures, even though many of their plants and flowers are imaginary or highly stylized. The pictures also reveal that Minoan women enjoyed considerable respect and freedom—far more so than in later cultures. Wealthy women are shown in places of honour and others mingle freely in a crowd watching a religious ritual. Women could also become priestesses and played important roles in religious ceremonies.

On a more mundane level, the Minoans had elaborate and efficient drainage systems which remained unsurpassed until Roman times. All the big houses had indoor lavatories and bathrooms. The Minoans were also skilled at engraving as is shown by their exquisite seal stones (right). Seal stones were a

La Parisienne
This famous Minoan face is named La Parisienne because of her upturned nose and pert expression. She was probably a goddess or priestess presiding at some religious rites. In paintings women were often depicted in positions of honour and playing an active role in society.

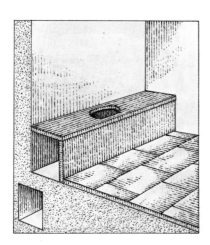

Sanitation
Minoan lavatories (above) were remarkably like modern ones. They were usually inside and were flushed with a pitcher of water.

Rain water and waste were carried away in clay or stone pipes (below). The conical shape was designed to help maintain the water pressure.

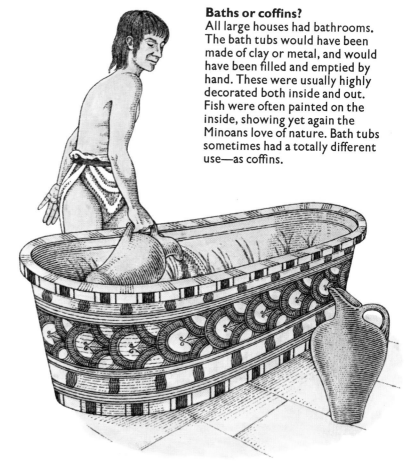

Baths or coffins?
All large houses had bathrooms. The bath tubs would have been made of clay or metal, and would have been filled and emptied by hand. These were usually highly decorated both inside and out. Fish were often painted on the inside, showing yet again the Minoans love of nature. Bath tubs sometimes had a totally different use—as coffins.

means of identifying property; a lump of clay set over the fastening of a box or a jar was stamped with the owner's personal seal. They could be made into signet rings or worn round the neck or wrist.

Early seals were made of soft materials like ivory, gold or silver. As cutting and engraving tools improved, harder materials like rock crystal and amethyst were also used. Cheap seals were made of serpentine, fired clay or glass. Early designs were simple and were chosen largely for their magic properties, possibly to protect their property. Pictures of animals, particularly strong ones like bulls and lions, were popular as were divine figures. As cutting techniques improved more elaborate designs were engraved. Some later seals have such intricate pictures that it seems impossible that they were done without magnification. Crystal lenses have been discovered that may have been used as magnifiers. Some late seals have elaborate myth or ritual scenes on them, but many have purely secular pictures.

The Minoans could certainly write though they left no written history or literature—only tablets recording commercial transactions. There appear to have been at least four systems of writing, two hieroglyphic and two that used signs for each syllable—Linear A and Linear B. It is possible that the scripts evolved in Crete as there are no obvious ancestors. Except for Linear B, Cretan writing has not yet been deciphered.

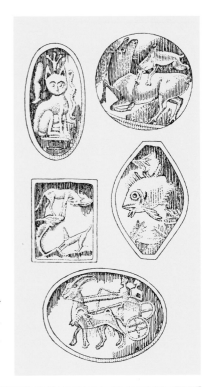

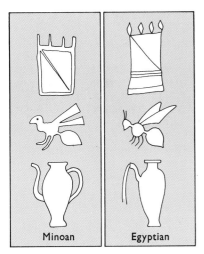

Minoan / Egyptian

Cretan writing
Although most of the signs in Cretan hieroglyphic script (above) bear no resemblance to foreign scripts some seem to be derived from Egypt. A few others seem to be reminiscent of early writing in Mesopotamia.

The two closely related Linear scripts developed by simplification from the earlier hieroglyphics. Of all the Cretan scripts only

Linear B has been deciphered. An Englishman, named Michael Ventris, concluded that it was an early form of Greek, but not all scholars accept this conclusion. Linear A, used up until the end of the palace period, 1450 BC, is thought to be a Semitic language. The disc showing a mysterious hieroglyphic script was discovered at Phaistos and dates from about 1600 BC.

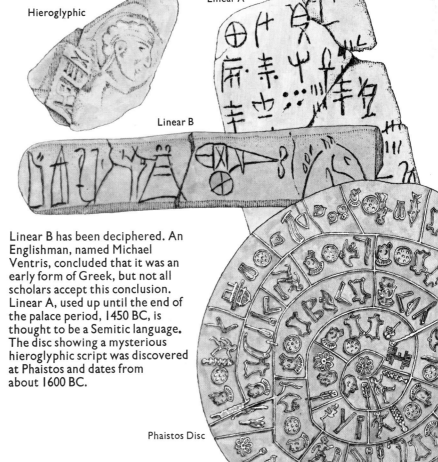

Hieroglyphic

Linear A

Linear B

Phaistos Disc

A dangerous pastime
Here are some athletes bull-leaping
in the courtyard of the palace of
Knossos. The man standing behind
the bull is ready to steady the girl
as she lands. There is plenty of
room for spectators round the
sides of the courtyard. They are
protected by a strong wooden
fence. The girl wears a man's
short kilt. It would have been
impossible to leap in the elaborate
skirts usually worn by Cretan
women.

Bull-leaping fresco
This fresco (below) of a bull-leaping
scene was found in the palace at
Knossos. In this picture the white
figures appear to be women
dressed as men.

The bull games

The central courtyard was the focal point of the palace at Knossos, with the rest of the palace buildings radiating outwards from it. The imposing entrance on the west side would have been the one used for ceremonial occasions: the religious and secular events that took place in the courtyard. Several of their religious ceremonies seem to have been celebrated in games and sports.

The Minoans probably held athletic contests much as the later Greeks did, and they certainly boxed and wrestled. Boxing may have been a religious sport but it was very savage—the participants wore helmets and knuckle-dusters. A clay model of a woman on a swing with doves on the supporting poles suggests swinging was a fertility rite and the Minoans celebrated occasions like sowing or harvest with processions, singing and dancing. These celebrations may well have taken place in the courtyards.

Bulls played an important part in Minoan religion. This is clear from the frequent appearance of bulls in pictures and on seal stones, from the bull's horn symbol on pillars and walls in the palaces and from the importance of the bull in legends. According to one legend, Minos was the son of Zeus who, in the form of a bull, seduced Minos' mother, Europa. Minotaurs appear on many seal stones and it may have been a Minoan deity, in which case the Minotaur legend may be rooted in fact. We do not know if human sacrifice was practised in Minoan Crete, but it is possible that when Minoan power was at its height, the Minos did compel the Athenians to send people to Crete to be sacrificed to a bull god. Certainly altars have been found and animals, if not humans, were sacrificed in the central courtyards.

The most spectacular ceremony that took place in the courtyards was bull-leaping in which daring young athletes, both men and women, somersaulted over a charging bull. To do this they grasped the horns of the bull and somersaulted as it tossed them into the air over its back. Sometimes the athletes leaped off a large block of stone. The chances of being killed or injured were great—one vase from Ayia Triadha shows a man impaled on a bull's horns. But it was not intended that either bull or athletes should be injured during the performance, although the bull may have been sacrificed after the contest. Pictures of bull-leaping show dappled, piebald and skewbald bulls, so they were probably domestic animals though doubtless very fierce nevertheless! Many people watched the amazing spectacle from behind a stout wooden barrier round the edge of the courtyard. The significance of this important rite is obscure.

15

Religion and death

Minoan religion was not one of fear but of rejoicing, festivity and dance. It seems that the most important deity was a goddess, probably of fertility. Less important was the male god, a god of vegetation who died and rose again like the plants. In autumn as the plants withered people mourned his death and in spring they celebrated his new life. The Minoans also had animal-headed figures which resemble Egyptian gods.

There are no elaborate Minoan temples, shrines were small and simple—one room with a bench for statues of the goddess and offerings. The largest was a three-roomed shrine surrounded by a huge wall at the top of Mount Juktas. The Minoans felt their deities were specially present in high places and in caves, and pilgrims would come there to pray. They left human figures there to represent themselves in constant attendance. These have their hands to their foreheads—the Minoan attitude of worship. Model animals were also left as substitutes for sacrifices.

Statues and shrines
The statue (top) is the snake goddess. Snakes were sacred because they shed their skin—the idea of death preceding new life. The other statue is her attendant.

Shrines were often in caves (left). Stalactites and stalagmites were sacred, the distinctive downward-tapering shape of Minoan pillars may be intended to imitate stalactites.

Worship of the dead
This clay model (above) from a large circular tomb near Phaistos, shows two people bringing offerings to two couples seated in front of altar-like tables. They may be gods if it is a shrine, otherwise ancestors.

The Minoans certainly believed in some kind of life after death because they made offerings to their dead. Some tombs had an altar outside for sacrifices, and the remains of clay vases for food and drink have been found around altars, at the entrance and inside tombs. The picture (below) is a reconstruction of an early round tomb with people bringing offerings for the dead. During the early and middle Minoan period the dead were buried in collective tombs which were used over many generations. The tombs were either carved out of limestone or built above ground, and were sometimes more than one storey, rectangular or circular. Caves were sometimes used for burial.

The Minoans rarely cremated their dead. They trussed up a body with the knees to the chin and laid it like this on the floor of the tomb. Sometimes they squeezed it into one of the large jars used for storing oil. From about 1600 BC, they began to use oblong coffins made of clay, limestone or wood if they were rich.

Coffin of a prince
Possibly this sarcophagus (right), from a tomb near Ayia Triadha, once held the body of a prince. It was carved out of a block of limestone and is beautifully decorated. On the side shown here the dead prince receives offerings of a boat and two bulls. The boat may be for a journey to the Minoan heaven. On the left of the panel some women prepare to sacrifice a bull and two goats while a man plays on some pipes.

17

A working city

Gournia was a coastal fishing town built on a hill. Like so many Minoan towns it had no fortifications. It was first inhabited around 3000 BC but did not become important until 1650 BC. It was burnt down in 1450 BC but a few houses were built on the ruins and it was not finally deserted until 1200 BC.

The town was a hive of industry. It had a factory to process oil or wine from the olives and grapes grown in the surrounding countryside. Carpenters had workshops making wooden columns, beams, shelves and floors for houses. They also made boats, carts and sedan chairs. Casting bronze to make tools and weapons was another important industry in Gournia. Engravers carved designs on tiny seal stones, potters fashioned fine vases and women spun and wove woollen cloth and linen. Like a modern town, Gournia had a shopping arcade and a market in the piazza near the governor's house. Here fishermen sold their catch and farmers came in from the outlying countryside to sell produce.

The seventy or so houses in Gournia were crammed tightly together. Poor people lived in cramped one-storey houses with a few small rooms, the wealthy had houses several storeys high. Craftmen's workshops were often on the ground floors with their living quarters above.

The streets were paved with stone and were narrow (less than two metres wide) and twisting. Most of the streets radiated out from the town centre but there were some ring roads. In places the streets sloped steeply and there they were built into steps. Goods had to be carried on pack animals. The wealthy were carried through the streets in sedan chairs and possibly litters. The poor walked.

To the south of the town was a governor's house which, like the palaces, had storerooms and a courtyard. To the north of this was a small shrine with a path leading to it from the main street.

Wine press?
This is believed to be a wine press. The grapes were placed in the jar with a spout, where they were trampled, and the juice flowed into the lower bowl.

Overflow runnel

Shallow Vat

Sunken *pithoi*

Workshop of the Aegean

The Minoans' taste for elegance and beauty was matched by their craftsmanship. They worked in stone, all kinds of metals, faience—glazed earthenware—and ivory. In addition to the household industries of spinning and weaving, making wine and olive oil, they also excelled at pottery and engraving.

Stone vases were made in most parts of Crete from 2500 BC onwards. These were any size from miniature palettes and bowls for mixing and holding face paint to the giant *pithoi*. Minoan craftsmen used simple but laborious methods hollowing vessels out of stone, but the more complicated shapes, like narrow-necked vases, were made in several pieces and fitted cleverly together.

From 2000 BC gold and silver, copper and bronze were in regular use. The Minoans also made some exquisitely delicate gold and silver jewellery. Bronze was being used for armour and tools, and polished bronze discs with carved wood or ivory handles made fine mirrors. Ivory, imported from Syria or Egypt, was used extensively for seals, combs, figurines, little boxes and inlays. Sometimes ivory work was decorated with gold leaf. A beautiful gaming board nearly three feet long was found in the palace at Knossos. It was made of ivory, plated with gold and inlaid with rock crystal and faience.

Pottery was being made by the Minoans from earliest times. Early pottery around 3000 BC was clumsy and decorated quite simply. Only slightly later Vasiliki pottery from 2500–2200 BC, called after the site in which it was found, had begun to take a more extravagant shape—like the long-spouted jugs. They had a mottled effect produced by holding burning twigs over the painted surface. When the palaces were built and their workshops opened,

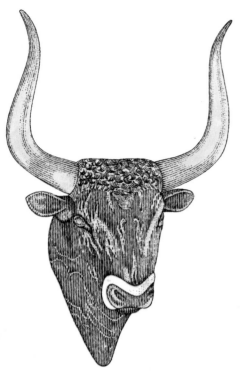

Bull's head vessel
This magnificent bull's head made of black serpentine was found in the 'Little Palace', northwest of Knossos. It is a ritual drinking vessel. It was filled at the top of the neck and was emptied through a hole in the mouth. This particular vessel is beautifully made with golden horns and eyes of crystal.

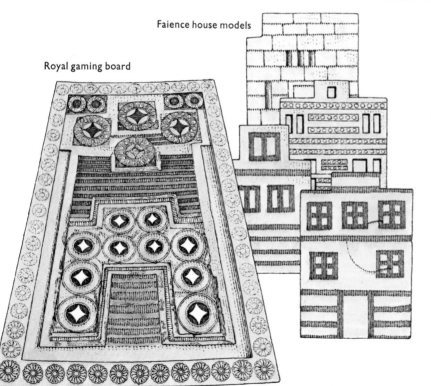

Royal gaming board

Faience house models

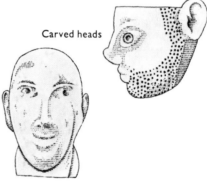

Carved heads

Minoan crafts
These objects give an idea of Minoan life: the fact they enjoyed gaming—the 'Royal Draught Board': the sort of houses they lived in from these tiny faience models, about 3 cm. high, from a mosaic frieze: and from these superbly carved faces what the people looked like.

skill in pottery-making developed rapidly. It was during the first palace period 2000–1700 BC that the potter's wheel was introduced and the Kamares style of very delicate pottery could then be made. On this eggshell-thin pottery they designed colourful patterns of white, yellow and red on a black background.

During the second palace period 1700–1400 BC a new style emerged of spirals and naturalistic designs of reeds and flowers. This again illustrated the Minoan love of the natural world in pottery, as in wall painting. About the same time a distinctive marine style came into fashion—remarkably lifelike octopuses, dolphins and starfish swimming against a background of seaweed and rocks. This was the finest of Minoan pottery and from this point as the Minoan civilisation declined, so did their pottery, the patterns became more abstract, the designs more stylized, and the quality deteriorated.

Golden artefacts

The Minoans mastered most of the gold working techniques known today, such as repoussé (pushing out a design on the reverse side of a thin sheet), filigree and granulation. On the right, two gold pendants, one of a god (top), the bottom one in the shape of two bees. The circlet (middle) was probably worn in the hair. The splendid gold cup on the left has a repoussé design of a bull being captured using a cow as a decoy.

A wealth of styles
Pottery from 3000 BC (I), the extraordinary spouted design, 2500-2200 BC (2 & 3), the colourful thin-walled pottery, 2000-1700 BC (4), then the lovely plant designs, 1550-1500 (5) and finally the realistic marine style 1500-1450 BC (6).

21

Trade across the sea

The Minoans were self-supporting for their basic needs, unlike the Egyptians who had to import timber, or the Mesopotamians who imported stone. On the contrary the Minoans had a surplus of stone, timber, olive oil and wool, amongst other things, and almost certainly exported them. However, Crete had no natural supplies of tin and little copper, so the Minoans imported these to make bronze. It was probably this that drove them to trade; copper came from Cyprus, tin from central Europe or west Italy.

As Crete lacked precious metals and stones, most imports were luxury items. Some foreign, particularly Egyptian, manufactured goods have been found in Crete, as have Minoan goods been discovered elsewhere. Magnificent goldwork has been found in the royal tombs on the Mycenaean mainland exemplified by the cup found at Vaphos near Sparta.

Minoan pottery was in great demand and was Crete's major manufactured export—Minoan pottery was the finest in the world of that time. As money was not in use, goods were either exchanged for others or paid for with an agreed weight of gold, silver or pieces of bronze in the shape of ox hides.

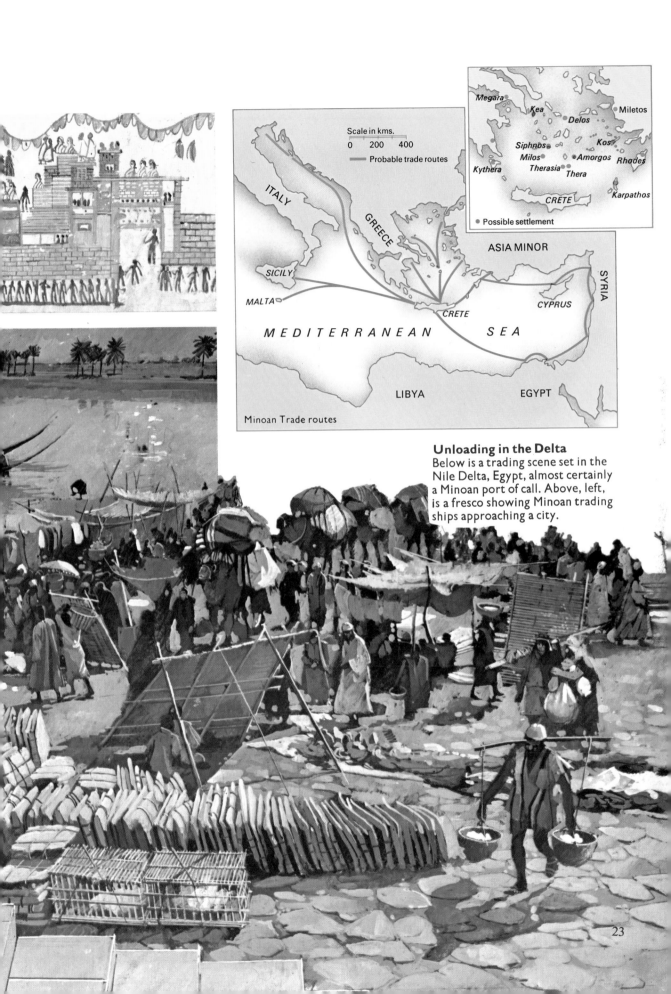

Scale in kms.
0   200   400
— Probable trade routes

Megara
Kea
Delos
Miletos
Siphnos
Kos
Milos
Amorgos
Rhodes
Kythera
Therasia
Thera
CRETE
Karpathos

• Possible settlement

ITALY

GREECE

ASIA MINOR

SYRIA

SICILY

CYPRUS

MALTA

CRETE

M E D I T E R R A N E A N   S E A

LIBYA

EGYPT

Minoan Trade routes

Unloading in the Delta
Below is a trading scene set in the
Nile Delta, Egypt, almost certainly
a Minoan port of call. Above, left,
is a fresco showing Minoan trading
ships approaching a city.

Naval supremacy

Pirates
Pirates probably came from the other Aegean islands and from the southern Turkish coast, but no one knows for sure. The Minoans may have recruited Carian mercenaries from south west Asia Minor to row their boats and fight. In a battle the opposing ships would have come alongside each other and soldiers would have fought hand to hand with swords and shields.

Although nominally peace-loving, the Minoans were the first great sea power. More than 1000 years after the demise of their culture, their naval power was still legendary among the Greeks. The Minoans gained control of the Aegean through their navy, which was probably not organised, judged by modern standards, but certainly had many ships. They were powerful enough to protect themselves against foreign invasion and to clear the South Aegean of pirates. But the Minoans were probably not above a little piracy on their own account! Nevertheless their power kept the Aegean relatively safe for trade.

Minoan power is attested by the fact that they colonised many of the surrounding islands, such as Thera and Rhodes. They also settled at Miletos in Asia Minor and may even have had colonies on the Greek mainland. They may sometimes have peacefully infiltrated local populations, but it is likely that at least some of the colonies were taken by conquest. Minoan confidence in their own supremacy at sea is reflected in their coastal towns, many of which were built on low lying land without fortifications to protect them.

Many Minoan boats were small enough to draw up onto a beach or anchor in shallow water, but some may have been 30

metres long. They had one mast with a square sail for long journeys, and paddles or oars. The Minoans are thought to be the first people to build boats with keels and many of their ships had more than one deck. Boats were steered by a big oar, or pair of oars, at the back.

From about 1600 BC Minoan warships probably had rams, but most fighting was done hand to hand with short swords and daggers. To defend themselves the Minoans used huge shields in the shape of a rectangle or a figure of eight which covered a man's body from head to foot.

Weapons
Minoan arms and armour were made of bronze, although helmets and corselets could be made of leather. The figure-of-eight shields (1) consisted of layers of bull hides. Rapiers with jewelled hilts (2) gradually gave way to shorter slashing swords from 1600 onwards (3) with horn-like projections on the hilts. The axe (4) is from an engraved sword blade, and was probably used as a defensive weapon. Other weapons were spears, slings and bows.

Minoan sea power
This fresco, only recently discovered on Thera, is rare pictorial evidence for the Minoans as a major sea power. Seven metres long, it shows a variety of galleys engaged in both warlike and peaceful pursuits.

Catastrophe

About 110 kilometres north of Crete lies the craggy volcanic island of Santorini, or Thera; once a Minoan colony. Around 1500 BC the volcano became active. Some experts believe there was more than one explosion, and it was probably an enormous one about fifty years later that proved so disastrous to Crete. We cannot be absolutely certain as to the causes responsible for the rapid collapse of the Minoan civilisation, but Thera must have been a major contributing factor.

Apart from wiping out the colony on Thera itself, the explosion caused havoc in the northern and eastern parts of Crete. The north-west wind carried clouds of volcanic ash over Crete and covered the land with a layer ten centimetres thick in places. This severely damaged agricultural land, killing crops and making the east of the island impossible to cultivate for many years.

The explosion caused part of Thera to collapse and the sea rushed in to fill the gap left by the expulsion of volcanic lava. This created enormous tidal waves over 180 metres. Travelling at 350 kph they must still have been about 90 metres when they hit Crete soon after the explosion. They swept over the coast

Destruction of Knossos
It has not been conclusively proved as to what finally led to the destruction of Knossos. It seems to have suffered extensive damage in about 1450 BC as a result of Thera eruptions, after which it was rebuilt, but finally about 1400 BC, it was destroyed by fire—a tragic end to a peace-loving and sophisticated culture.

devastating the north and east of the island.

The fleet, upon which the Minoans depended for power and wealth, must have been shattered. Initially, the south and west of the island, protected by the mountains in the centre, and Knossos, being inland, were spared the worst of the immediate impact. But soon after Knossos and the rest of the island also suffered as a result of the eruptions on Thera. What with the noise of the explosions, the darkness caused by clouds of volcanic ash, suffocating gases and raging fires, it is no wonder the Minoans thought the fury of the gods was unleashed upon them.

After the eruption the Minoans may have started to repair their ruined land. Crete lost a great deal of wealth through the destruction of her farming land and with the loss of her fleet, trade was no longer viable, and she was without protection. The Minoan culture was declining; the palace workshops at Knossos still produced fine goods, but elsewhere workmanship was poor—possibly due to poor facilities after the catastrophe.

The nation was considerably weakened, morale was low, Crete was now an easy prey for invaders.

Changing roles

Knossos seems to have fared slightly better than the rest of the palaces and towns in Crete; the rest were destoyed and abandoned. Knossos was the only one to be partly rebuilt and reinhabited—but not by Minoans alone. On the Greek mainland was a growing civilization—the Mycenaean. It seems that the Mycenaeans took advantage of Crete's weakened position to infiltrate the Minoan island and extend their power. At the same time Minoan influence was waning with Minoan colonies on Thera and Kythera abandoned.

Many changes in Crete suggest the presence of Greek conquerors—not least the Linear B script which is thought to be Greek. New houses built at this time and new pottery shapes reflect ideas current on the Greek mainland. These new Cretans were obviously a warring nation—many Linear B tablets are lists of weapons, military scenes were painted on the walls of the palace and tombs of warriors containing many weapons have been found in the region of Knossos. It is generally accepted that they were Mycenaeans—a more aggressive people dominating Greece at this time.

The conquerors did not rule for long in Crete. The last palace at Knossos was finally burnt down in about 1400 BC. This may have been the work of new invaders, perhaps rival Mycenaeans, or Minoan rebels. Native Minoan culture persisted in pockets in outlying areas until 1100 BC. After this it faded out; the inhabitants of once proud cities fled for refuge to the mountains to escape the raiders and pirates who once again began to terrorise the eastern Mediterranean.

After 1450 BC
The pottery above dates from 1450 BC; gone is the naturalistic style of the Minoans, to be replaced by the stylized form of the Mycenaeans. Below is a Mycenaean suit of armour, found at Dendra.

A legend uncovered

Minoan Crete

Minoan Crete has captured the imagination not only through its reappearance in history, but also through the beauty of its culture. The impression gained from the Minoan paintings and their artefacts is of a carefree, happy people with a marked love of beauty. The Minoan culture contrasts markedly with the grandiose Mycenaeans and their aggressive, warlike culture that followed. When Arthur Evans excavated the palace at Knossos (below) he put a 1000-year chapter back into history. Some of his conclusions have since been proved inaccurate and his reconstruction of the palace at Knossos has been criticised, but for all that it allows the visitor to Knossos to experience for himself something of the glory that was Minoan Crete.

Minoan civilisation is surrounded by an aura of romance. The fact that it remained forgotten and quite unknown for so long and the amazing circumstances of its discovery give it a fairytale quality. To the Greeks, the Minoan age was a golden age, a lost paradise, and this linked it in modern minds with the Greek legend of Atlantis. So the twentieth century has added a few of its own to the legends surrounding the Minoans. Stories about the Minoans are hard to combat because the evidence is not conclusive and can be interpreted in many ways. There is no written history to follow. While the Minoans kept meticulous business records, they do not appear to have kept a record of anything else. So while their art is highly original, their literature, philosophy and religious writing is non-existent; at least there are no traces of it so far.

Researchers are further hampered by the fact that they cannot read much of the writing that has been found, and even the legible script, Linear B, is not universally accepted as Greek. So for all that has been discovered about Minoan civilisation it is still clouded in mystery and many of the conclusions drawn are speculative—well-informed guesses in most cases, but guesses nonetheless.

Index

Ariadne, 5
Artists, 12
Asia Minor, 5
Athens, 5

Baths, 12
Boats, 6, 24, 25
Boxing, 15
Bronze, 20, 22
Bulls, 5, 13, 14–15
Bull's horns, 9, 11, 15

Carpenters, 18
Caves, 5, 16, 17
Copper, 20, 22
Courtyard, 15
Craftsmen, 9, 18
Cyprus, 22

Death, 17
Double axes, 9, 11

Egypt, 13, 20, 23
Engraving, 12, 13, 18, 20
Evans, Sir Arthur, 5, 9, 11, 30
Export, 6, 22

Frescoes, 12, 14, 22, 25

Gold, 20, 21, 22
Gournia, 18

Gods, 16

Hieroglyphic script, 13
Homer, 6
Houses, 6, 7, 12, 18, 20

Ivory, 20

Knossos, 5, 7, 8, 9, 11, 14, 15, 20, 27, 29, 30

Labyrinth, 5, 11
La Parisienne, 12
Lavatories, 12
Linear A, 13
Linear B, 13, 29, 30

Minos, 5, 8, 15
Minotaur, 5, 15
Mycenaeans, 29

Navy, 5, 24

Olive oil, 7, 9, 22

Palace, 5, 6, 7, 8, 9, 11, 14, 15, 20, 21, 29
Phaistos disc, 13
Picture, 11, 12
Piracy, 24
Pithoi, 9, 20

Pottery, 20–21, 22, 29

Religion, 11, 15, 16
Religious ceremonies, 15

Sealstones, 12, 13, 15, 18
Shields, 25
Shrines, 16
Silver, 20, 22
Snake goddess, 16
Storerooms, 6, 11, 18
Swords, 25
Syria, 20

Thera, 26, 27, 29
Theseus, 5
Throne room, 10, 11
Tombs, 17, 22
Trade, 22, 23, 24, 27

Vasiliki, 20
Ventris, Michael, 13
Volcanic explosions, 5, 26

Weapons, 25, 29
Women, 11, 12
Workshops, 9, 18, 27
Writing, 13
Wrestling, 15

Zeus, 15